Francisco's Fabulous Friends

An adventure from A to Z

by Taco Matthews

WINDRAD PRESS

Francisco's Fabulous Friends
www.franciscothefrog.com
Text © 2011 by Taco Matthews
Illustrations © 2011 by Taco Matthews
All rights reserved

No part of this book may be used or reproduced in any manner whatsoever without written permission except in the case of brief quotations embodied in critical articles and reviews.

Windrad Press
An imprint of Pinwheel Books
Brookline, MA
www.pinwheelbooks.com

Library of Congress Control Number: 2011928721

ISBN-13: 978-0-9832577-2-1

Printed in the US

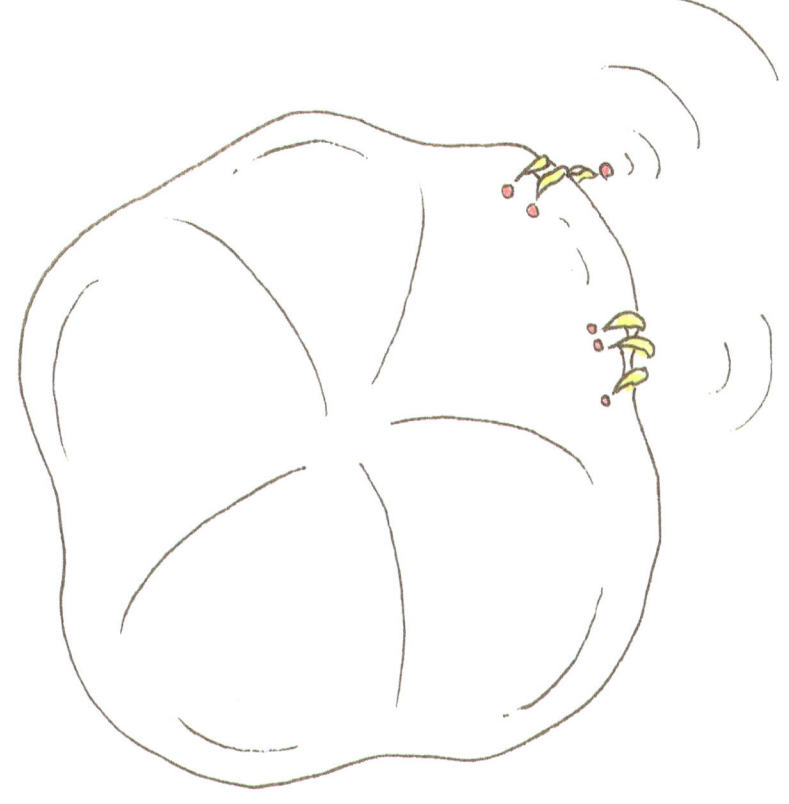

To Chris,

Lily and Momo.

Hello! My name is Francisco the Frog.

Let's go and meet all my fabulous friends.

ant

Anna

artistic

Anna the ant is artistic.
She is always painting and drawing.

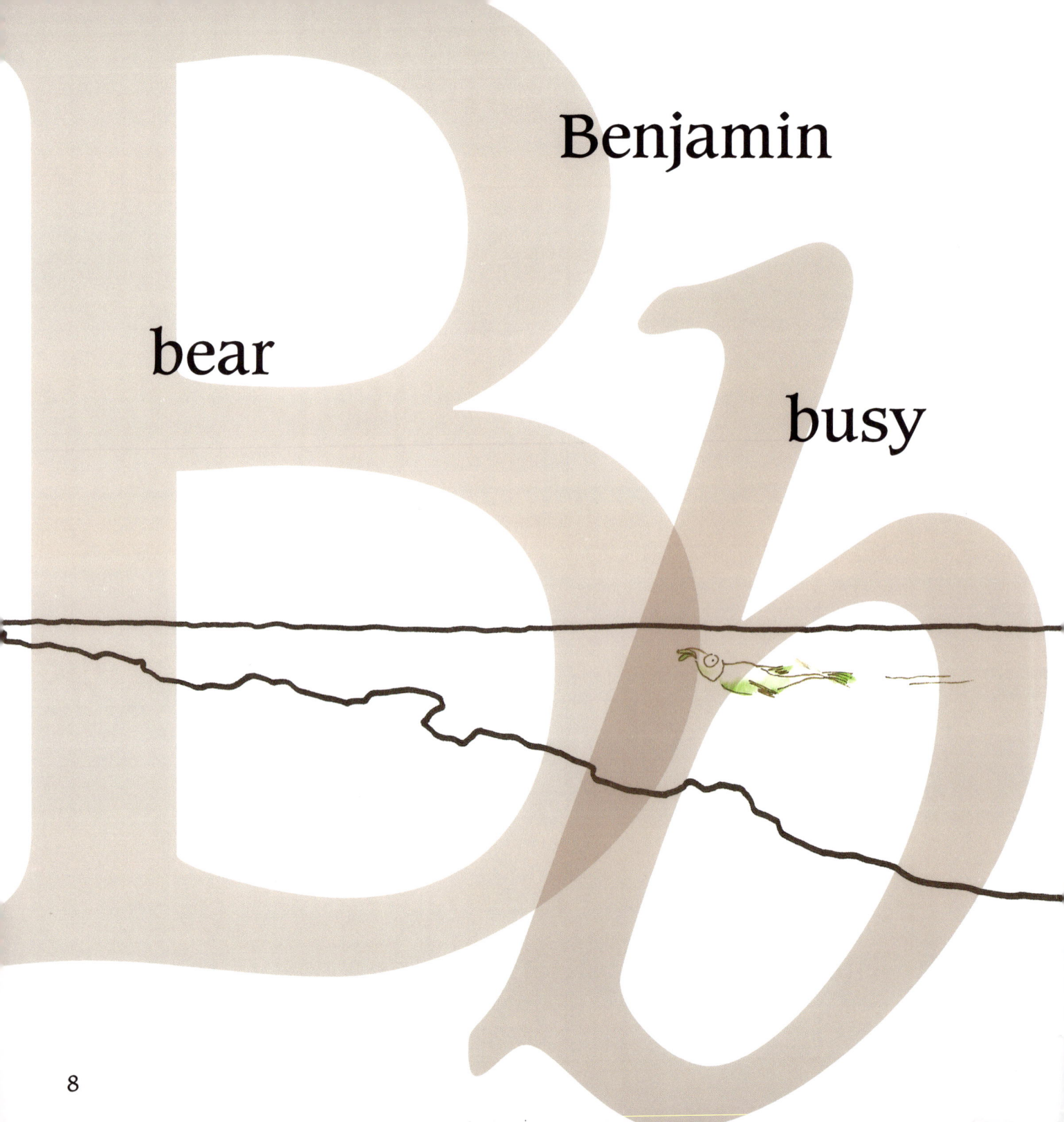

Benjamin

bear

busy

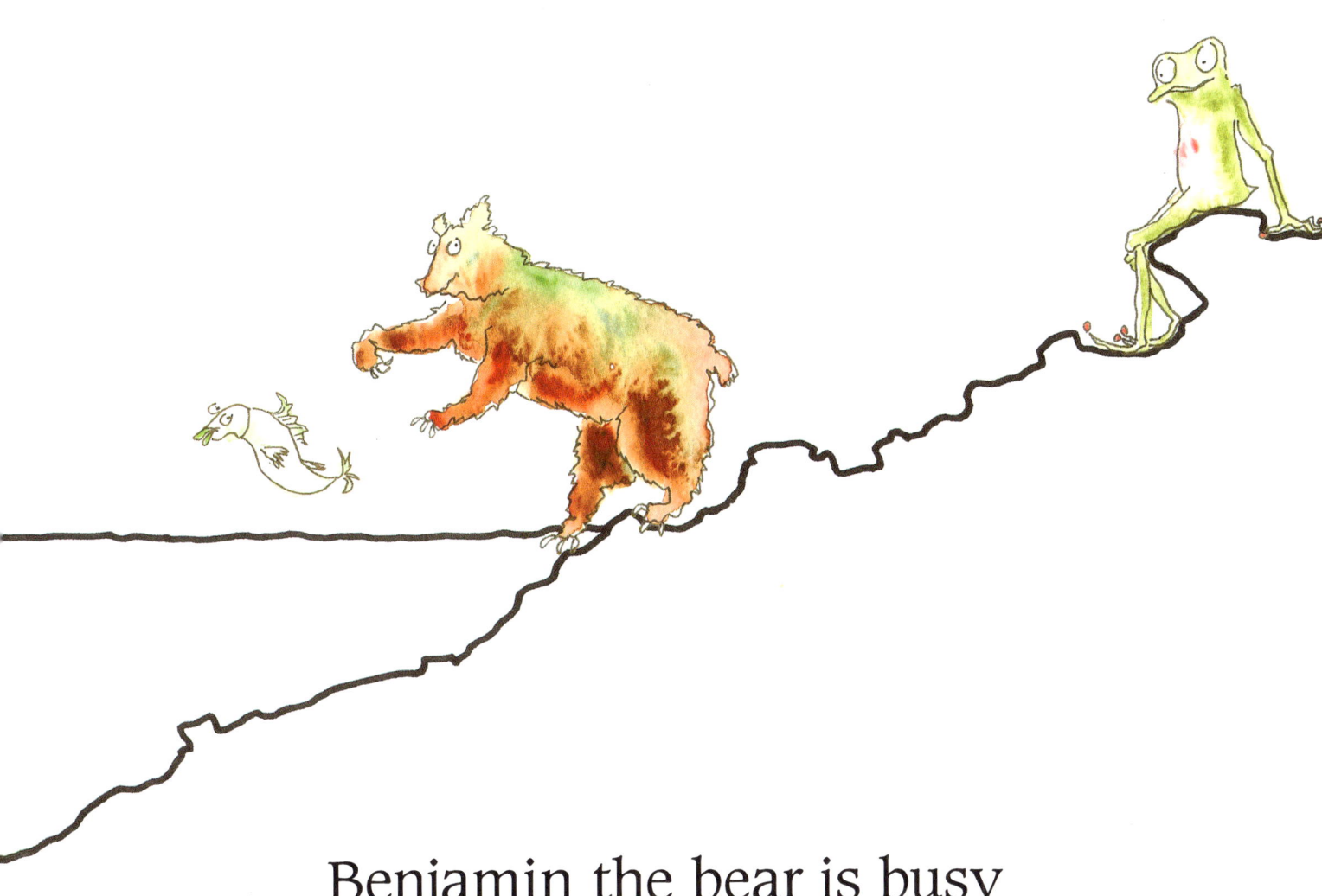

Benjamin the bear is busy
catching fish for the family dinner.

cat

Carmen

curious

Carmen the cat is curious.
Will she find any treasures today?

dragonfly

Dominic

dizzy

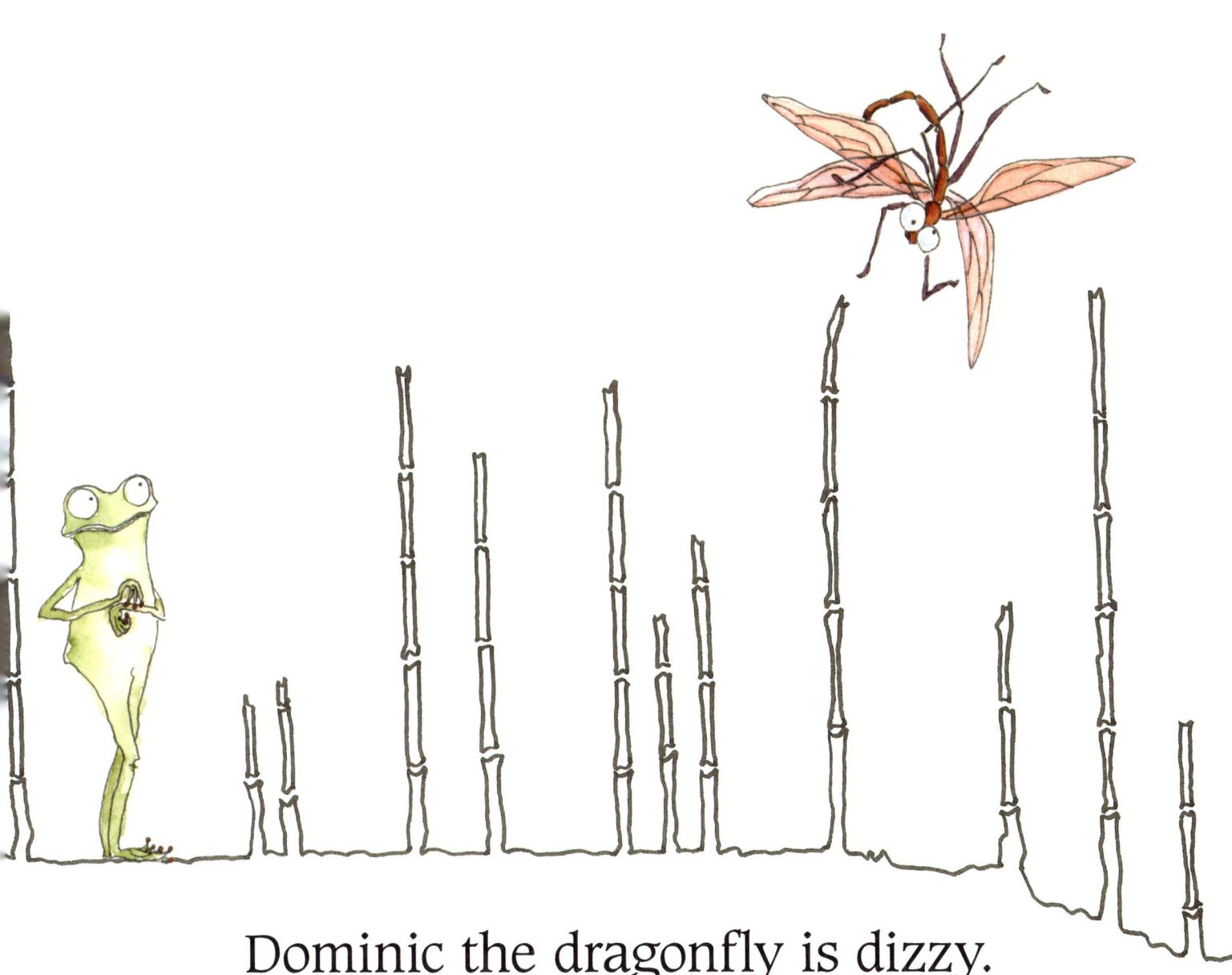

Dominic the dragonfly is dizzy.
I think he needs some help!

emu

Emily

excited

Emily the emu is excited.
She is about to come out of her shell!

fish

Frances

fashionable

Frances the fish is fashionable.
I wonder if she wants to dance?

goat

George

grumpy

George the goat is grumpy.
I better not open the gate!

hen

Henrietta

hilarious

Henrietta the hen is hilarious.
She says you're upside down!

iguana

Ian

intelligent

Ii

Ian the iguana is intelligent.
I think he is writing a secret code!

Jj

jellyfish

Jerry

jolly

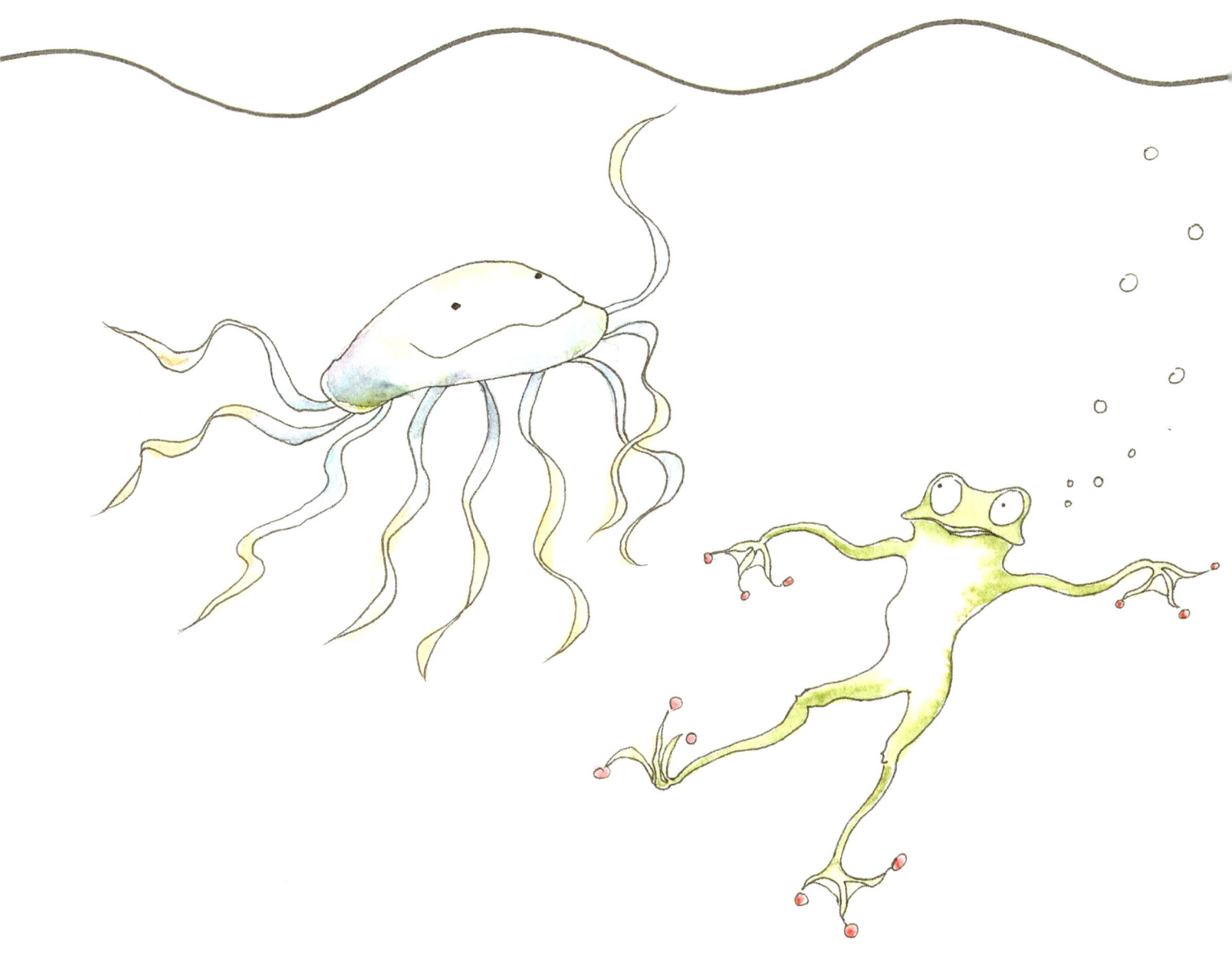

Jerry the jellyfish is jolly.
He is a jittery jiggler.

kangaroo

Katie

kind

Katie the kangaroo is very kind.
She brings me water when I am thirsty!

lion

Leo

lazy

Leo the lion is lazy. Do you think he is ready for his piano concert?

monkey

Maurice

mischievous

Maurice the monkey is mischievous.
Oh, oh, he is looking for trouble!

nightingale

Nicole

noble

Nicole the nightingale is noble.
I love her silky singing.

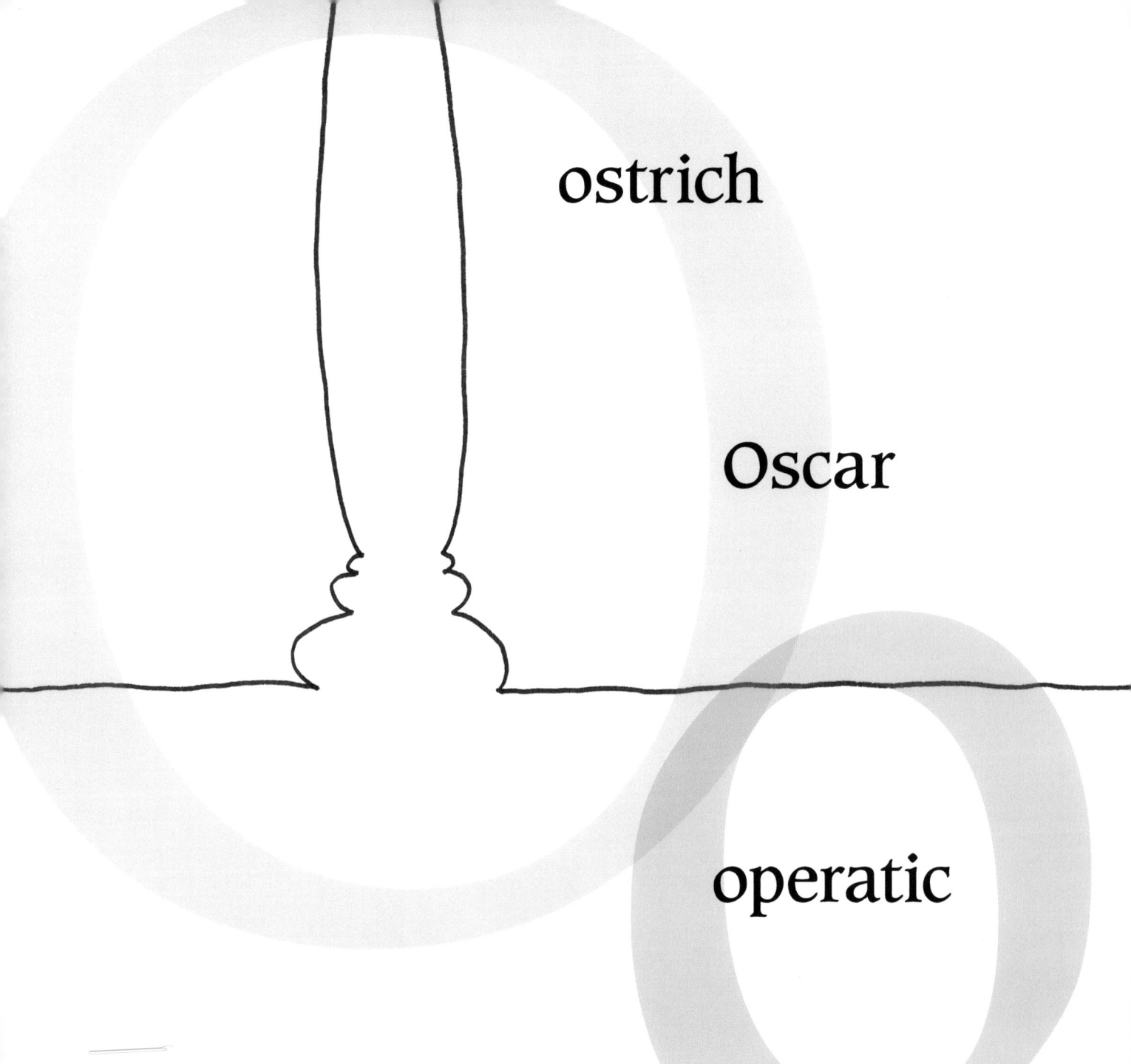

ostrich

Oscar

operatic

Oscar the ostrich is operatic.
He needs a spotlight, don't you think?

penguin

Patrick
Petra
Peter

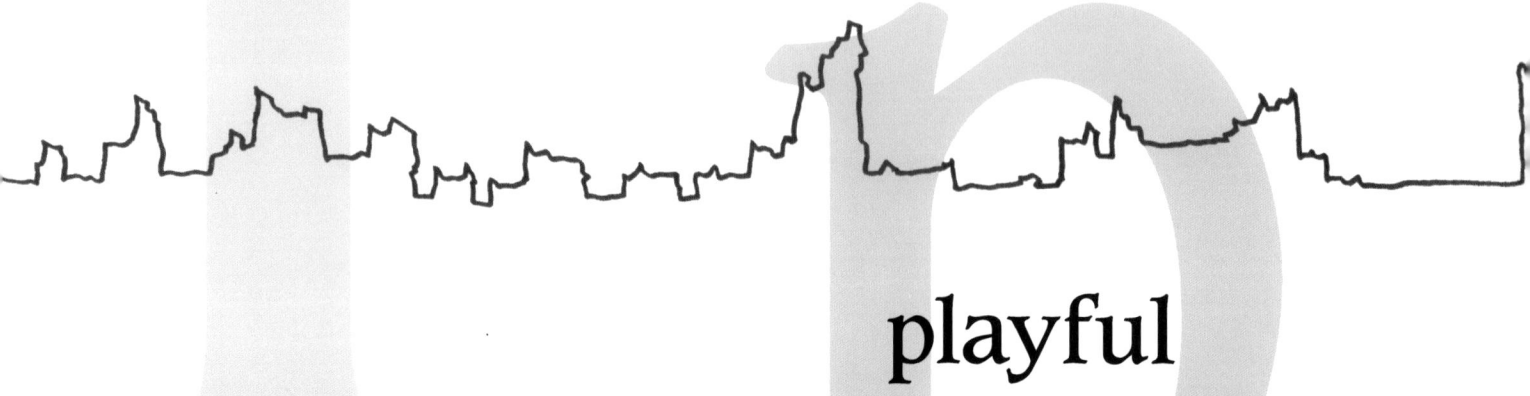

playful

Patrick, Petra and Peter the penguins are playful. Look at them playing hide-and-seek!

quetzal

Queenie

quiet

Queenie the quetzal is quiet.
I wonder if she has a secret?

rabbit

Rebecca

rushing

Rebecca the rabbit is rushing.
She can hop even faster than I can!

snake

Sally

silly

Sally the snake is so silly . . .
She likes to make snake pretzels!

turtle

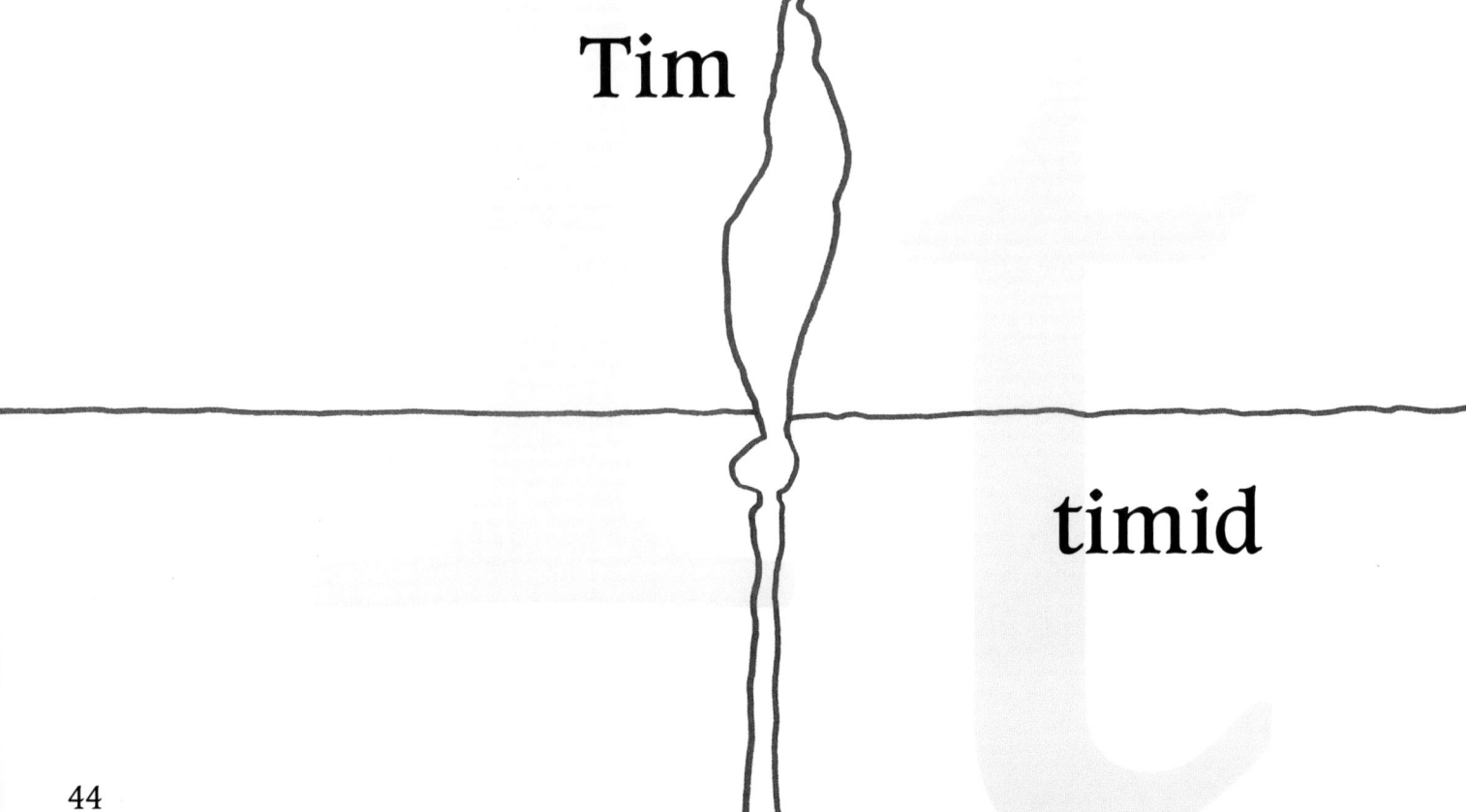

Tim

timid

Tim the turtle is timid.
I better not scare him!

unicorn

Ursula

unique

Ursula the unicorn is unique.
She can jump over the clouds!

velociraptor

Vincent

vanished

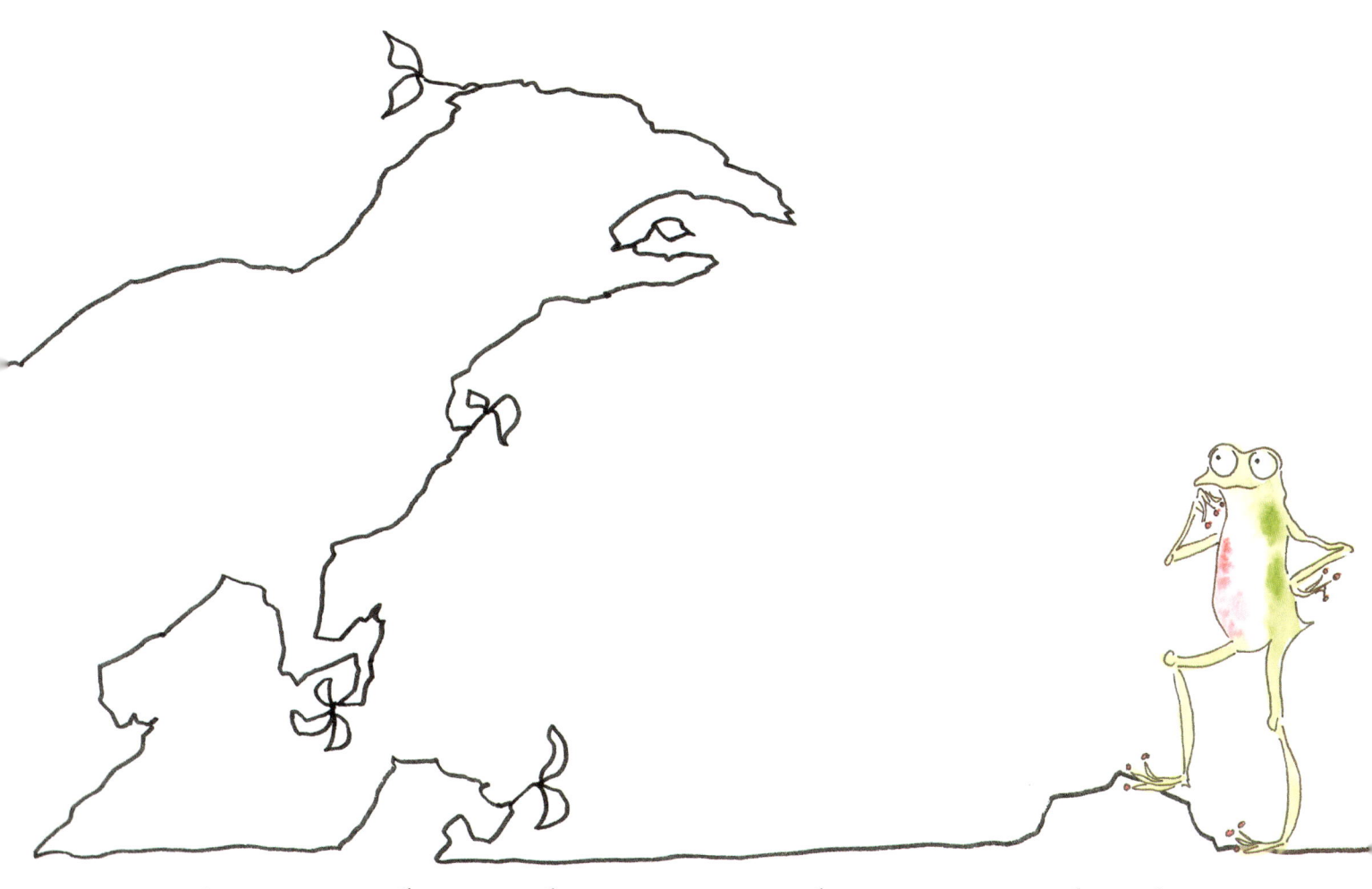

Vincent the velociraptor has vanished!
Was he really there or in my imagination?

wolf

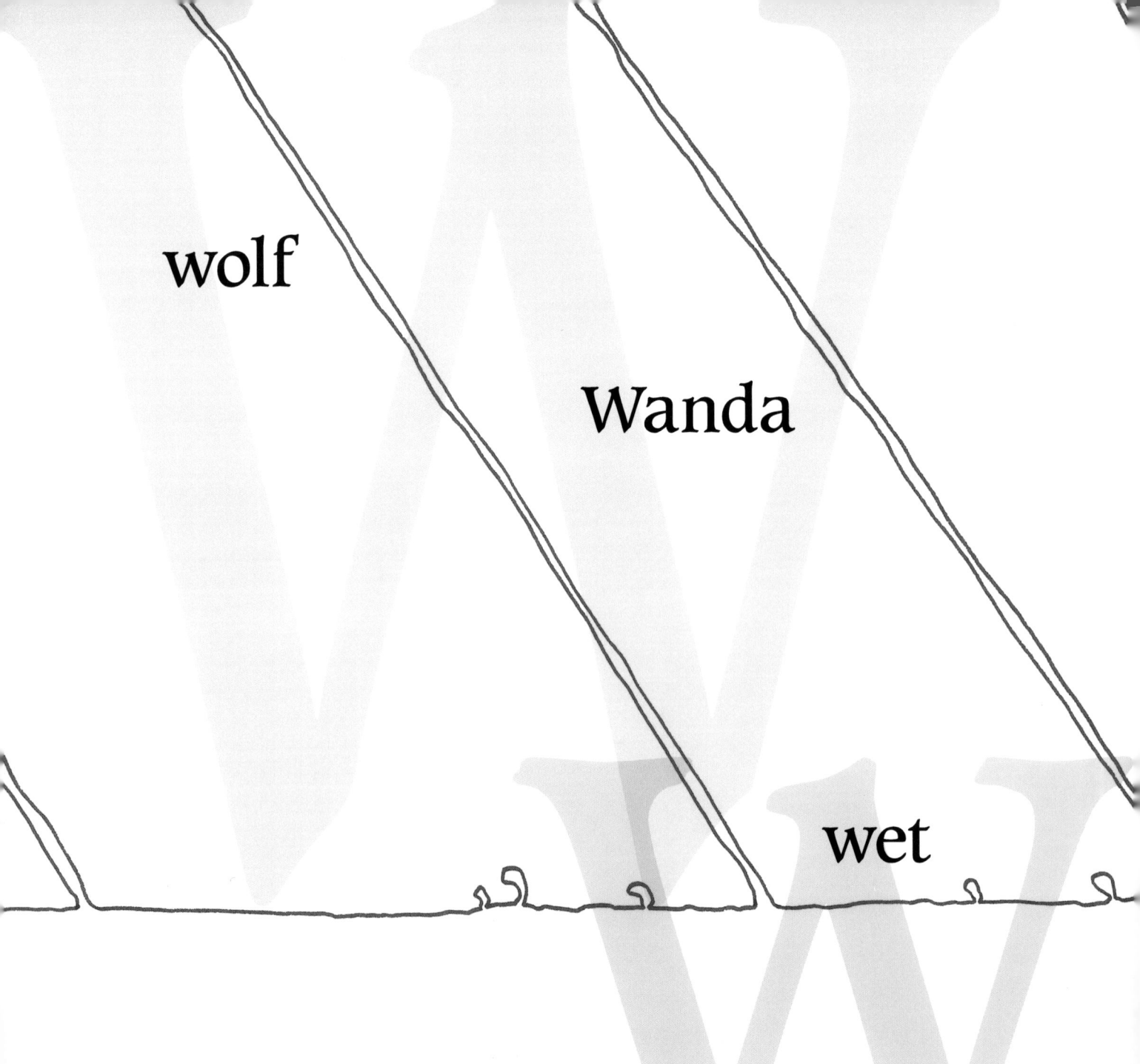

Wanda

wet

Wanda the wolf is wet.
Should I share my umbrella with her?

xerus

Xavier

xanthous

Xavier the xerus is xanthous.
Do you know what that means?
Let's look in the dictionary!

Xerus
[zeer-uhs]
African ground squirrel that has a spiny fur, very short ears, and a long tail.

Xanthous
[zan-thuhs]
Somewhat yellow; tinged with yellow.

yak

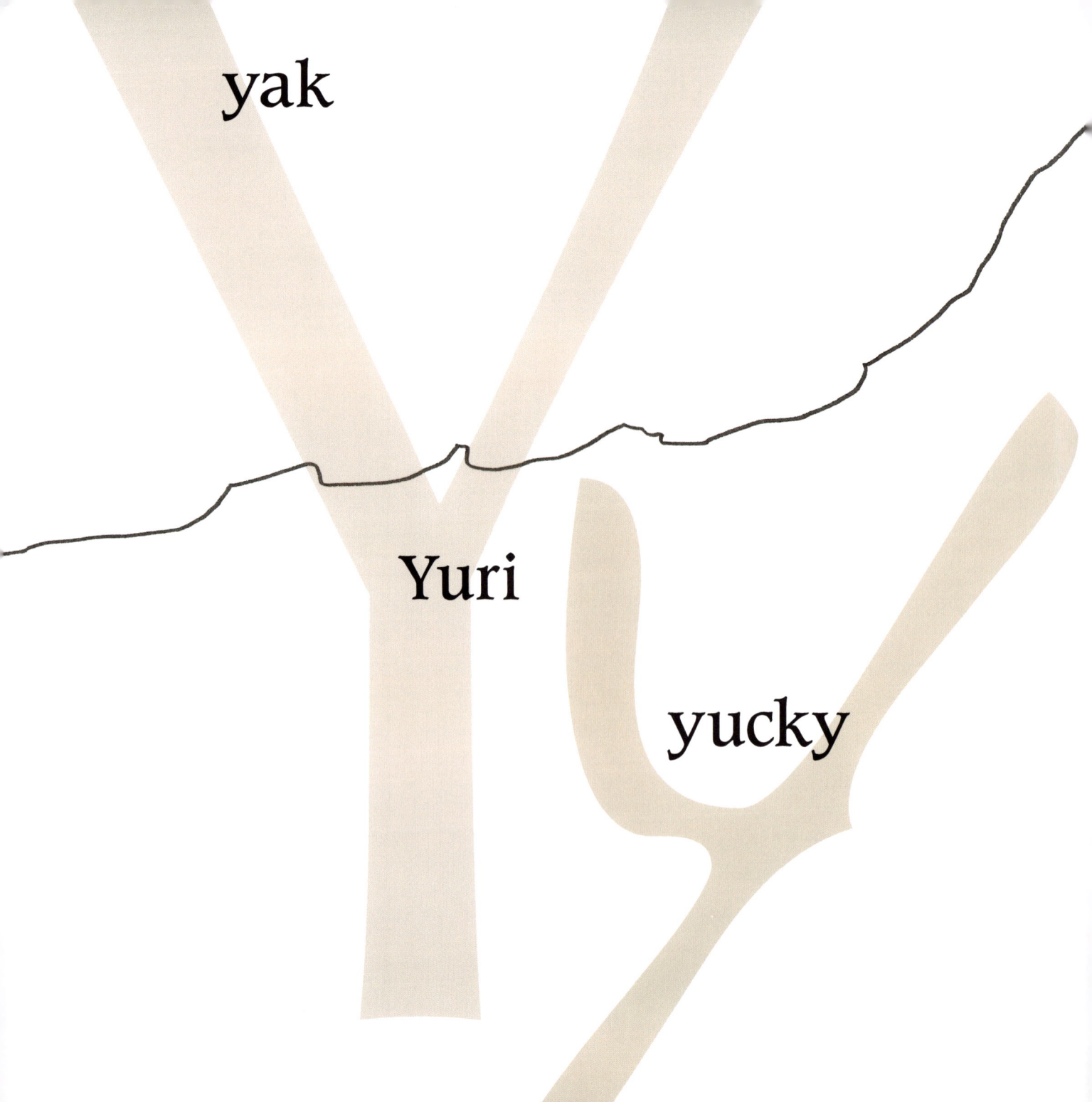

Yuri

yucky

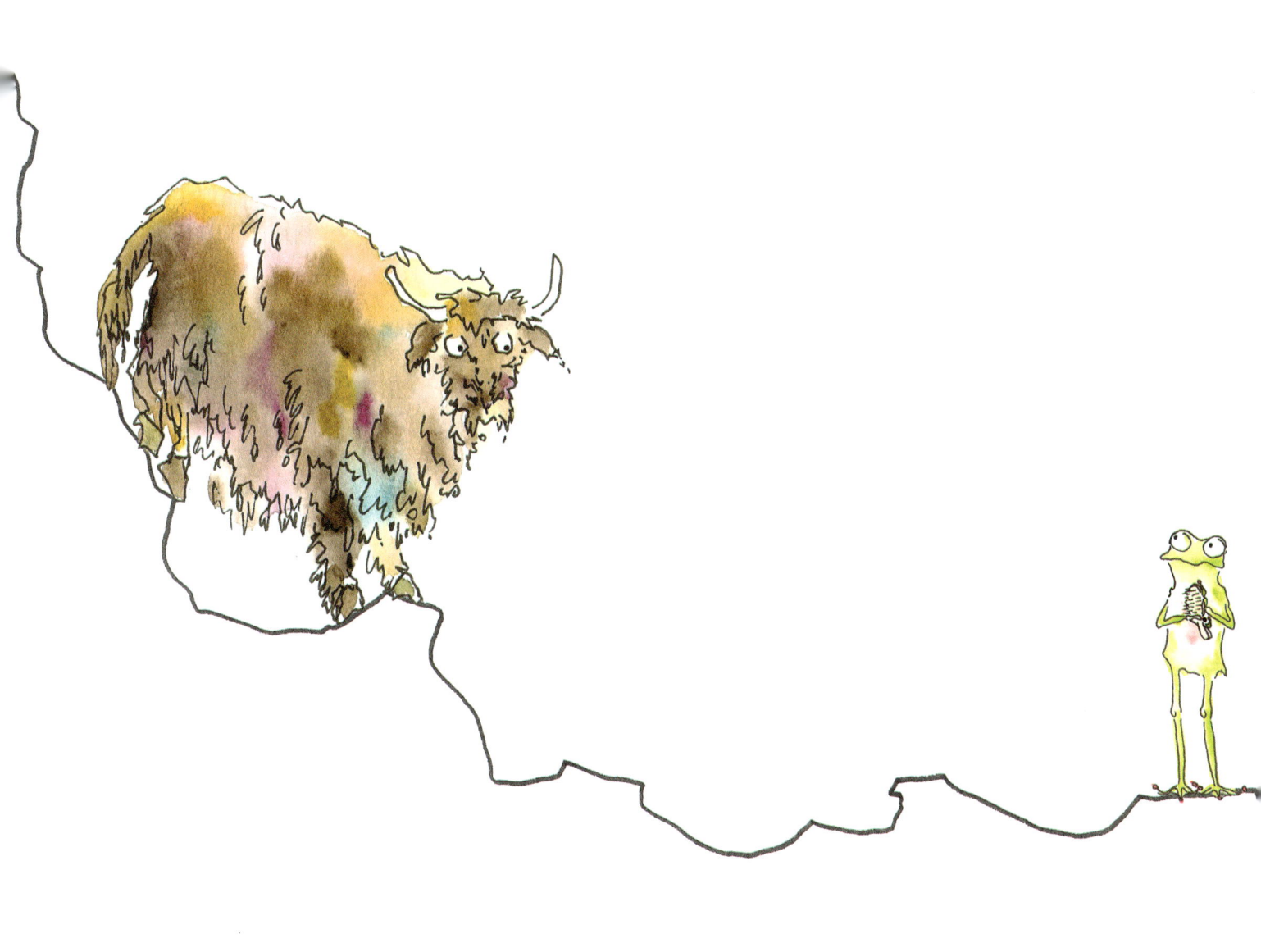

Yuri the yak is quite yucky.
I am glad I brought my hair brush!

zebra

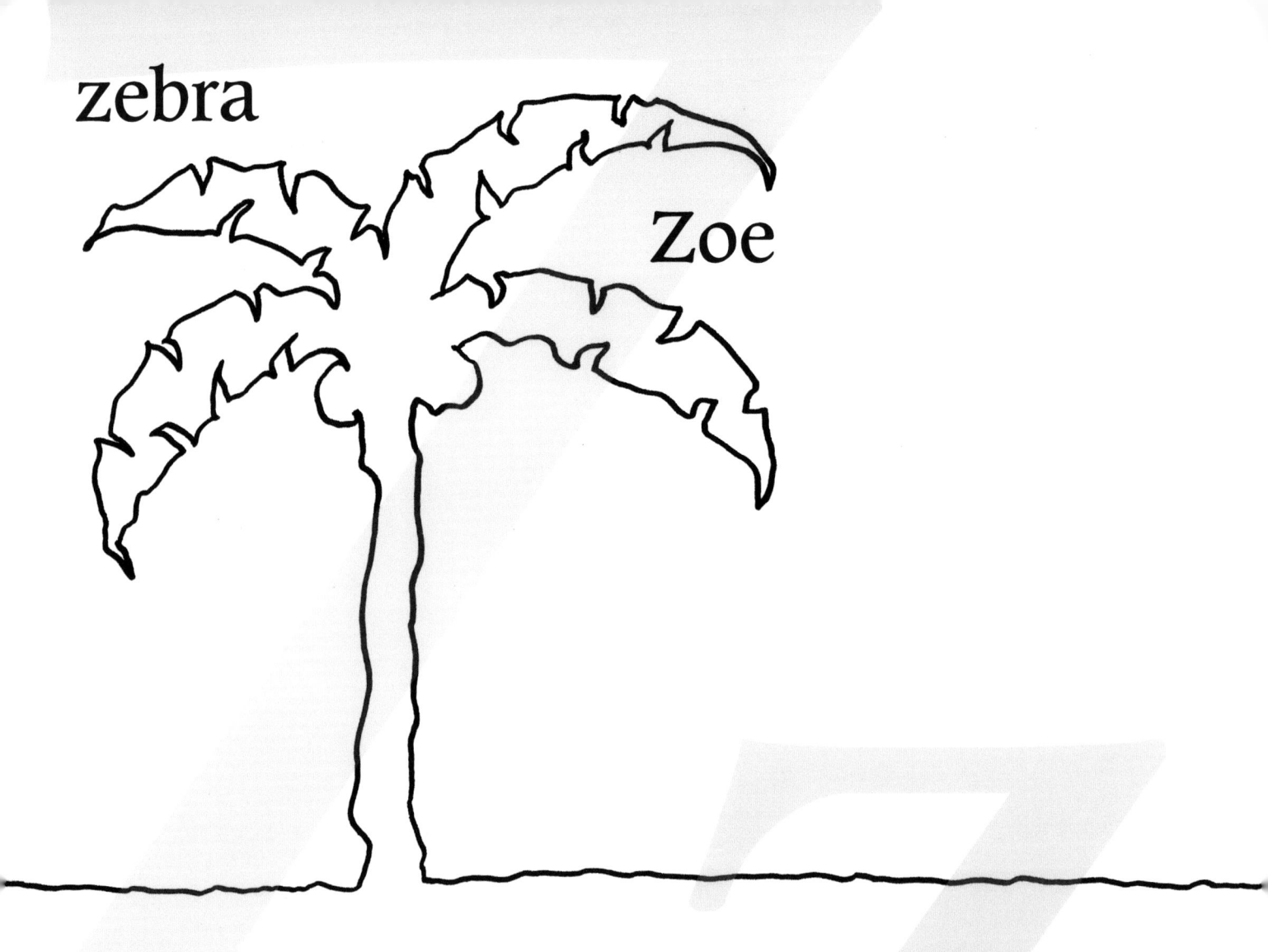

Zoe

Z-Z-Z

Zoe the zebra is . . . Z-Z-Z . . . sleeping . . .
I promise I won't wake her up!

Aa Bb Cc Dd
Ee Ff Gg Hh
Ii Jj Kk Ll
Mm Nn Oo Pp
Qq Rr Ss Tt
Uu Vv Ww Xx
Yy Zz

Now comes my favorite game! Can you match the letters with my friends?

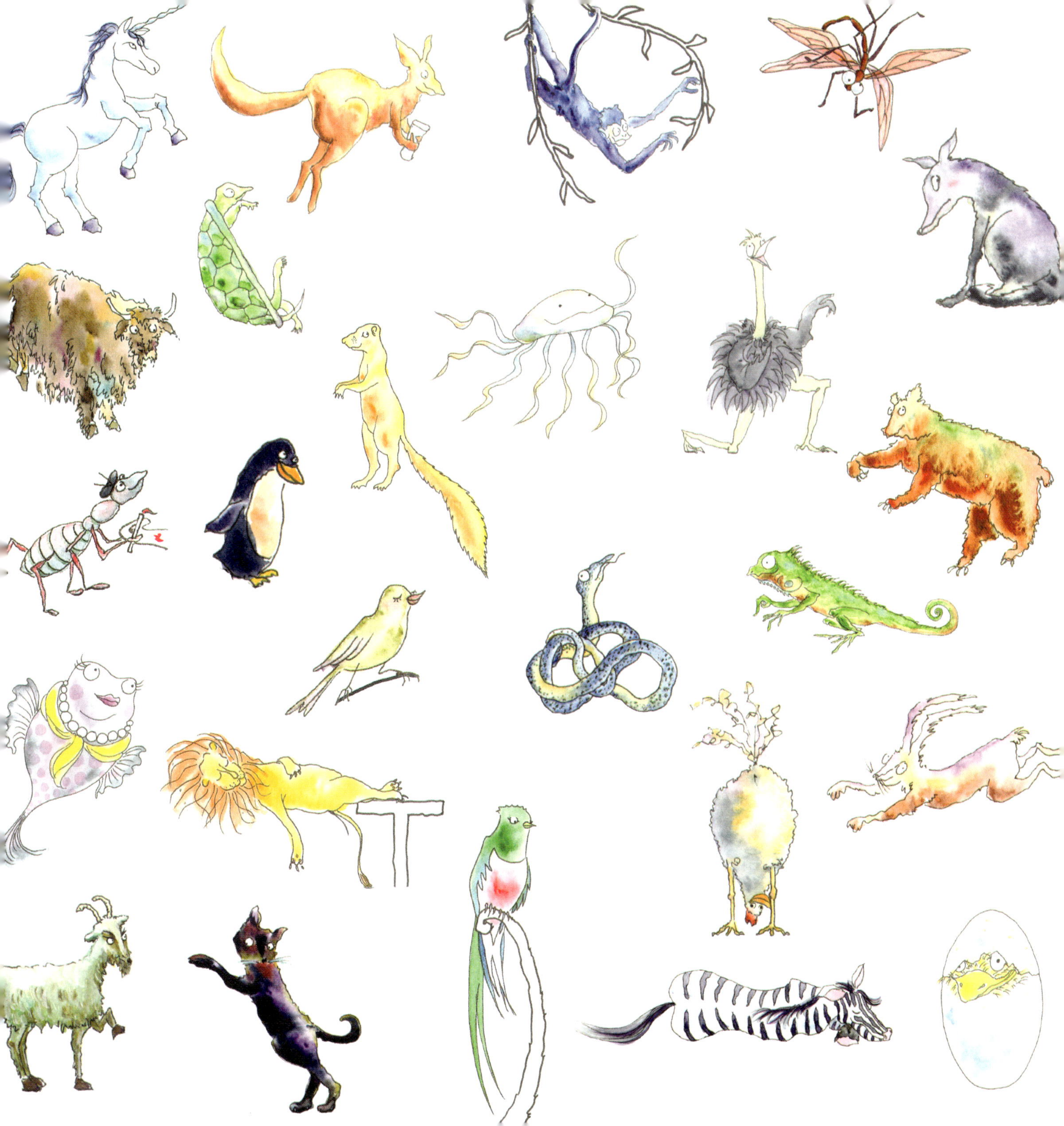

Goodbye!